* Basic Rules *

395

— · — · — · — Fold in the reverse direction of the dotted line. This is known as the "mountain" fold.

— — — — — Fold along the dotted line in the direction of the arrow. This is called the "valley" fold.

———— Cut

①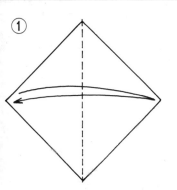

②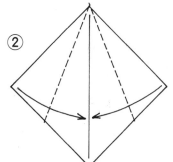

③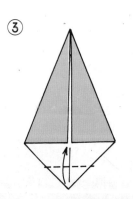

④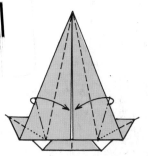

Turn it over.

⑤

⑥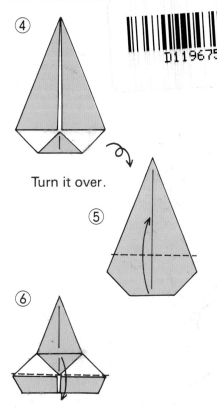

⑦ Turn it over.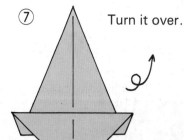

Pull both sides toward center.

⑨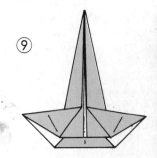

Turn it over.

Finished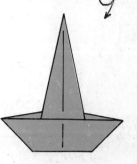

2

COASTER

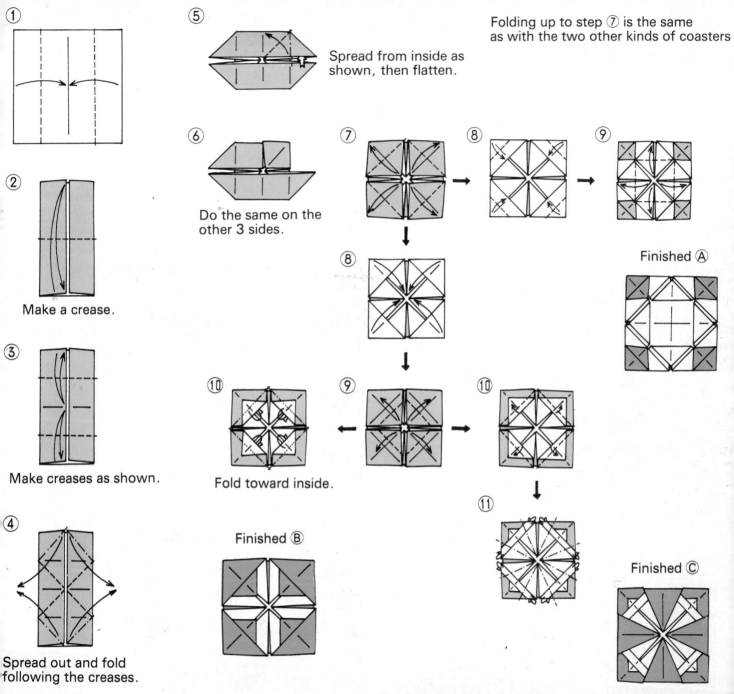

①

② Make a crease.

③ Make creases as shown.

④ Spread out and fold following the creases.

⑤ Spread from inside as shown, then flatten.

⑥ Do the same on the other 3 sides.

⑦

⑧

⑨

⑧

⑩ Fold toward inside.

⑨

⑩

⑪

Finished Ⓐ

Finished Ⓑ

Finished Ⓒ

Folding up to step ⑦ is the same as with the two other kinds of coasters

4

SNAIL

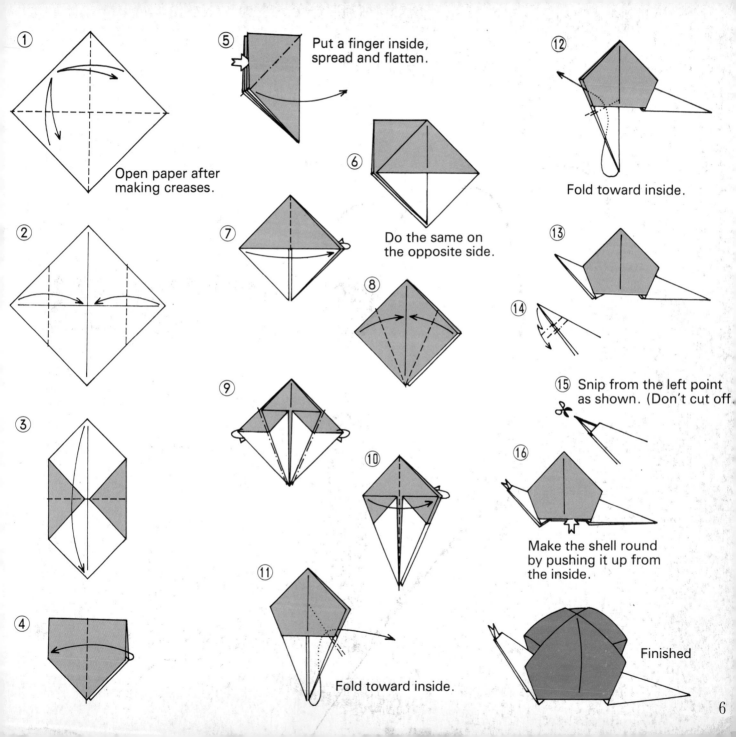

① Open paper after making creases.

⑤ Put a finger inside, spread and flatten.

⑥ Do the same on the opposite side.

⑫ Fold toward inside.

②

⑦

⑧

⑬

③

⑨

⑭

⑮ Snip from the left point as shown. (Don't cut off.

⑩

⑯ Make the shell round by pushing it up from the inside.

④

⑪ Fold toward inside.

Finished

6

LUNCH BOX, DISH, AND NAPKIN RING

See page 13.

① Make a crease.

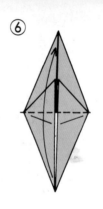
⑥

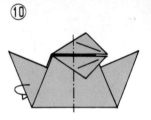
⑩

②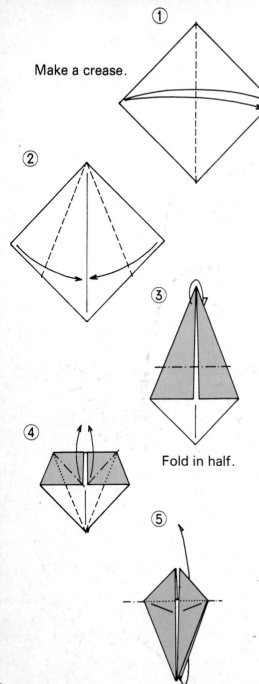

⑦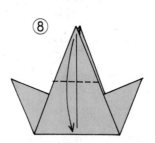

Pull the triangles out to
the sides as shown in step ⑧.

③
Fold in half.

⑧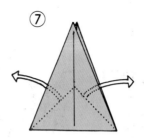

⑪

Draw eyes.

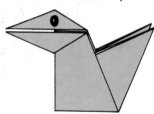

Finished

④

⑤

⑨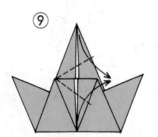

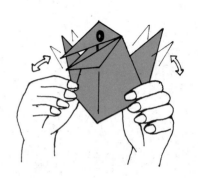

Hold it as shown.
When you move the wings apart,
the beak opens.

9

Follow steps ① to ⑤ for "TALKING CROW" on page 9.

①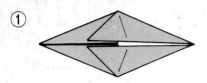

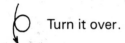 Turn it over.

②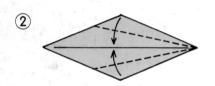

③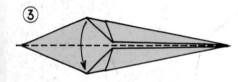

④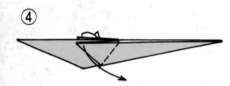

⑤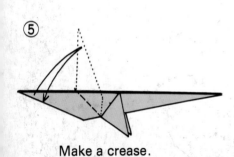

Make a crease.

⑥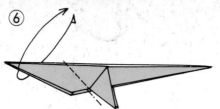

Fold up while spreading paper to outside.

⑦ 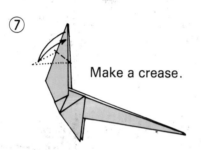 Make a crease.

⑧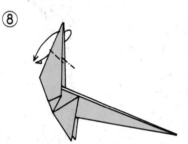

Fold down while spreading paper to outside.

⑨

Fold a "valley" and a "mountain" to make a face.

⑩

Fold toward inside.

⑪

Fold down toward inside.

⑫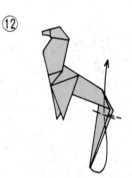

Fold up toward inside.

Finished

DOG

LUNCH BOX I

① ② ③ ④ Fold the other side in the same way as in steps ①–③. ⑤ ⑥ Open to form a bo[x]

center

II

Turn it over.

① ② ③ ④

⑤ ⑦ ⑨

⑥ ⑧ Fold the opposite side in the same way as in steps ④–⑦. ⑩ Open.

Finished I

Finished II

DISH

① ② ③ Turn it over. ④ ⑤ ⑥

Make creases as the lines show.

Turn it over.

⑦ ⑧ ⑨ ⑩ ⑪ ⑫

13 Make pleats in corners as shown (⑦–⑩). Turn it over.

Finished

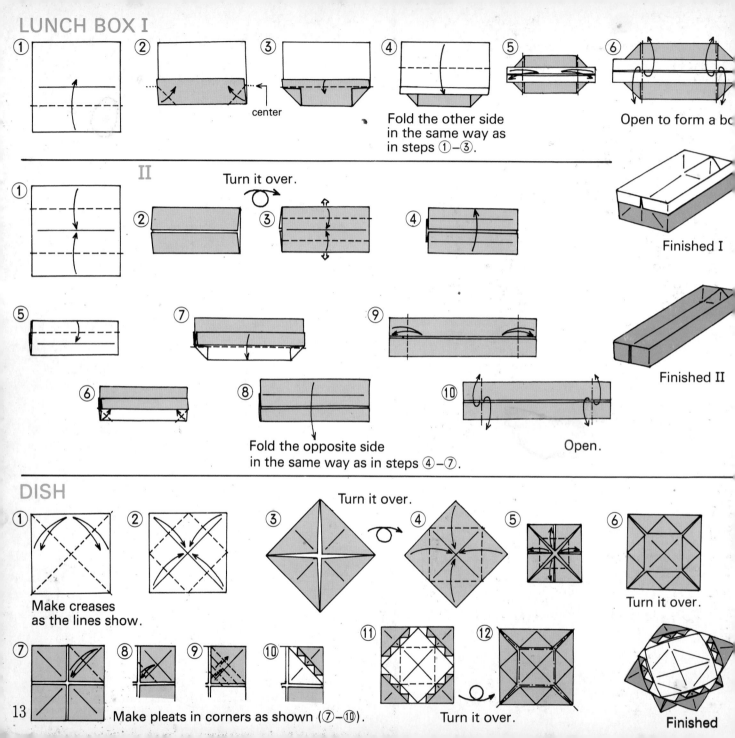